Parenting Teens

The Tug-A-War to Adulthood

Presented By

COACH P. KOFFE BROWN &
DFG PUBLISHING HOUSE LLC.

This book is written for informational purposes only. It contains general relationship information. This book is designed to assist with building healthy, strong, long-lasting family relationships. It is the thoughts, personal and professional opinions of the Authors. D. F. G. Publishing House LLC and the Anthologist/Author disclaim any responsibility for actions taken without first seeking professional advice or for misunderstandings on the part of the reader.

D. F. G. Publishing House LLC

Printed in the United States of America

ISBN: 979-8-218-01955-6

Book Design by P. Koffe Brown
Myles Adams- Brown
Maya Adams
Yasmin Brown

Please enjoy our publications titled:

"The Race to the Ring, The Seven Seas of a Successful Courtship."

"Why He Married Her and Played Me, Nine Secrets to What He's Thinking."

"Why He Married Her and Played Me, The Sequel."

"She Chose Him and Screwed Me, Nine Reasons for Her Decision."

"A Date with Destiny, I Gotta Have Him Although I'm Married to You."

"Transition, Going from a Good Life to a Great One!"

Coming Soon

"From Whorish to Wholesome, A Tale of Two Cities Housed in One Body."

CONTENTS

Acknowledgements

I want to thank you, the reader, for picking up this book and enjoying the pages. If it were not for you, then writing for me would be in vain. I certainly want to thank God for blessing me with this unique idea to bring the value of healthy relationships to the forefront of all our minds. Next, I must thank **LOVE** for leading me to have a desire to share this type of connection with another human being. I also must thank my parents for creating me and showing me the power of loving one human being for life! I have never seen two people fight so hard to lead a life that shows the magic of partnership, purpose, patience, persistence, and passion. You two are a real-life example that all things are possible in a relationship if you believe!

I would also like to thank the humans that I have created Myles, Maya, and Yasmin Mone't. The three of you push me to win. Thank you for being my children and my reason **WHY!** You guys are making me into a "**DOPE BILLIONAIRE MOM.**" I enjoy being your mother. It has made me a much better woman. I love you, and always remember that you are my greatest gift!

Finally, I would be remised if I did not thank the other contributing authors and the fantastic editor on this project. As I began to think and consider the pages of this book, your names came to mind. For some reason beyond my understanding, you said YES without hesitation. For this, your time and your talent, I thank you. It is a great honor to share the stage and these pages with your presence. Again, thank you to my readers. May this book grace your life and bless your family forever. Enjoy dears welcome to PARENTING TEENS!!

P.S. Thank you to the parents that raised me Bishop and Lady Arthur L. Adams Sr. I learned how to be a good mother from both of you. I am eternally grateful for good parents.

Love Is.......

Love is the one power that can transform all our lives. Love can create an environment that makes us come alive and be at ease. Love is a shelter from the rain of life. Love is past a feeling into purpose. Love leads and guides us into truth. Love covers all our human faults, frailties, and failures. Love outlasts anything and everything in life. Love does not know the grave; it remembers those who captured our hearts that no longer dwell here. Love is the master of meaning. Love is the passion that drives us to the arms of one another. Love is pure, purposeful, and painless. Love is the magic that reveals the meaning of why we choose one person over the other. Love is the perfect thing on earth. Love leads us to our purposed person and commands our undivided attention. Love arrests our hearts while captivating our minds. Love is the energy that wakes us up in the morning, and it is the same force that lays us peacefully to sleep at night. Love never fails. Love never changes. Love is consistent. Love is contagious. Love is captivating and calming. Love is beauty beyond one's body. Love is what we need to enjoy a perfectly imperfect person. Love is what brings a smile to our face while we dance away the night. Love is the laughter that we share while lying in each other's arms. Love is the exchange of spirit while connected to the soul of our commanded partner. We do not need love; we are LOVE because God created us, and He is LOVE. Love is EVERYTHING!

Welcome to "Parenting Teens, The Tug-A-War to Adulthood."

Introduction

————— ✦ —————

Parenting is the most challenging and rewarding job we will ever have in our lives.

Training up a child to become a healthy young adult takes a lot of time, energy and effort. The teen years have been documented as the ones that will make or break a parent. Yes, a parent!

Don't fret we are here to help you and your teen win. This book has come from my heart, through the writers' hands, and into your homes. Our prayer is that the strategies, tips and tools shared in this book bless your family forever. Know that if we made it parenting teens so can you. Please enjoy or presentation of "Parenting Teens, The Tug-A-War to Adulthood."

Wishing you the best,

Coach P. Koffe Brown

Coach P. Koffe Brown - Anthologist Visionary, CEO & Marketing Guru

What's the love of your life? For the speaker, certified life coach, and healing practitioner, P. Koffe Brown, it's empowering others to heal.

A proponent for living life with passion and purpose, Koffe's story is not much different from most of her clients. With astounding clarity borne from years of intensive work, Koffe has unraveled the impact of freedom in her life and recognized that her life's purpose revolves around supporting others in their journey to inner peace, wholeness, and love.

Koffe's combination of personal experience and professional skills compelled her to create *Destined for Greatness PAS* in 2003. Through inspirational speaking and coaching, Koffe takes clients on a transformational journey of healing and growth, all to incorporate a holistic approach to soul cleansing and deliberate change. She focuses on shifting relationship patterns, raising self-awareness, and channeling energies back to its true essence, one of divine spiritual love.

Driven by her mission to promote holistic growth, Koffe creates unique, powerful, and high energy experiences that delight others to take hold of their vision and put it into action. Embodying the essence of her core message, "Free your mind, and the past will soon be left behind!" Koffe contentedly fulfills her passion for serving others through coaching, writing, workshops, social media talk shows & live seminars.

An author, avid reader, lover of communication, and all things transformative, Koffe's mission is - and will forever be - to heal, inspire, and create change in the world, one heart at a time.

Please enjoy the amazing authors of this publication.

Janiqua Lache'a Bio

Janiqua believes in educating the whole child. It is her desire to create an atmosphere where students and staff can and will meet their full potential. Janiqua LaChe'a has been in the field of education for twenty years. Most of her years in education were spent with at-risk students. She has spent years making significant impacts on the lives of the students she has encountered. She received both her master's and bachelor's degrees from Prairie View A&M University (in radio and television/film broadcast and counseling & leadership). While working at her previous school, she started an all-female mentoring group, Cupcakes & Conversations, where she provided workshops on self-esteem building, etiquette, and poise. Janiqua LaChe'a is a proud member of Delta Sigma Theta Sorority Inc.

Feel free to connect with Janiqua LaChe'a on any of the following:

Instagram: Redwinediva_21
Facebook: Janiqua LaChe'a
YouTube Channel: Ms. Janiqua LaChe'a Jiles
Email: Janiquajiles@gmail.com

CHAPTER 1

Teens And Self-Esteem

By
Janiqua LaChe'a

———⋯✾⋯———

My Personal Quest
Patricia A. Fleming

For most of my life, I've been on a quest
To discover just who I may be,
Earnestly searching, day after day,
So desperate to recognize me.

I've felt moments of utter fulfillment
And moments I couldn't go on,
But I knew for the sake of my heart and my soul,
To succeed, I would have to be strong.

But the people around me seemed so lost themselves
That I feared I might be on my own.
But then there'd be someone who would reach out and help
And remind me I wasn't alone.

I've wanted so much to be happy,
To know what it was to feel peace,
And I thought if I finally felt sure of myself,
Then the pain and the struggles would cease.

But I've learned that this journey is endless;
The discoveries are fresh every day,
And no matter how much I may know of myself,
There'll be times I will still lose my way.

And as I've grown older, I truly believe
I may never know all I can be.
But the answers are not waiting out in the world
But have always lay right inside me.

We're all on this quest to discover ourselves,
Together but through our own ways,
Overcoming whatever may get in our paths,
So we can feel better someday.

But always remember not to stray far
From what matters and what's really true.
In this life you don't have to be perfect.
In the end, you just have to be you.

Over the years, I have worn several hats in my field of education. My role has gone beyond the classrooms. I have been a mother, aunt, nurse, counselor, and friend. I have seen students who struggle with fitting into a society where everything is centered on how many likes you can get on social media. This chapter is about your teens and self-esteem. I won't try to give you statics, facts, and data, because I'm no expert nor a biological mother. However, I am a passionate, dedicated woman and educator who has nurtured, cared for, fed, and loved my students past the halls of any schoolhouse and as if they were my own. I feel this alone makes me just as much a mother as if I had them myself.

You yourself, as much as anybody in the entire universe, deserve your love and affection, but try telling that to a teenager! Riddled with notions of self-doubt, loneliness, responsibility, and insecurity, their sense of self is lost. And when they think they're different, they don't think of celebrating their uniqueness; they don't see the people who accept them for who and what they are. All they notice is the person or people who don't. Lack of self-esteem is an issue that all of us face in today's society; however, this issue is particularly poignant, painful, and persistent in teens. Since we've all been there, it's imperative that we all come together to help them build up their sense of self, as their today and tomorrow, and even ours, for that matter, rests on their vulnerable shoulders.

Social media is a major outlet that plays a key role in the young lives of teens. Yes, social media is fun and even exciting as you sit and scroll through all the glamorous lives of the rich and famous. But a lot of our teenagers get caught up in the picturesque vacations, perfect video bodies, and fabulous clothes. (I must admit, hell, I do, too, sometimes.)

I know what you're saying to yourself. How do I help my teen have a healthier sense of self-love with social media at the forefront? However, social media is not always the source of self-esteem issues. Parents and caregivers, you, too, play an important role in forming how your child sees his or herself. You also give them confidence and the wings to succeed in many areas of their lives. Remember, the seeds we plant in our children can either cause them to wither or help them flourish. When you tell a child they are beautiful, handsome, smart, kind, and loving and can do anything their hearts desire, they will believe you. When you plant negative seeds, they will believe them too. As Scripture says:

Train up a child in the way he should go: and when he is old, he will not depart from it. (Proverbs 22:6)

It is important to make sure our teens have some kind of spiritual and emotional grounding. This will help them navigate throughout their high school and early college years. When they have a foundation of unconditional love, they are less likely to be bullied or feel worthless throughout their teenage years. They start to form opinions about how they view themselves and the impact of the words of those around them.

We must choose our words wisely when talking to our teenagers. We come from a culture that says, "It takes a village," and it definitely does. As an educator, I have tried to mold and shape the students I have encountered throughout my years in education. A simple kind word can be the catalyst for a young person with no self-identity and a lack of motivation. In my experience, I have connected with my students because of my genuine openness to love them where they are. The more interest I express in my student's well-being, the more responsive they are to being open with me. The vulnerability they show with me is evident when they reach out to me for support.

By establishing a space where they can create a foundation for growth, I help them learn the tools for emotional stability. I encourage students to keep an open heart and explore the possibilities of their joy by teaching methods of self-care and love. Although there is an easily accessible connection to the world through social media, students may feel intimidated to step out of their comfort zone in face-to-face situations. Social anxiety has formed in subconscious ways, such as hesitation to shake hands as a side effect of the pandemic/public distance. This is one of many ways that anyone, especially students, would question their approach to strangers and, in this case, fellow students and administrators.

It is imperative that I adjust to the times and exercise the most effective ways to support students in alignment with our current environment and society. One's words and support are most effective when they establish a connection with the target audience. These are as simple as a timeless "How are you?" or asking them to share their perspectives on viral media topics in hopes of sparking topics directed toward building morale.

In an article by Helena Lopez, she stated that when we do this, we show them that we care and they do make a difference. "Believe it or not, self-esteem affects their personality and relationships with their peers, as well as their attitudes, decision and problem-solving abilities, energy, creativity, and success in reaching goals."[1] The more things we can pour into them, the better off they are. Below are a few quick things we can do to improve teens' self-esteem:

- Allow them to be open and honest.

- Be an example of unconditional love.

- Don't make them feel unloved or unwanted.

- Encourage and support their dreams and efforts.

---

1 Lopez, Helena https://www.chs-ca.org/podcasts/transcript/self-esteem

- Let them know it's okay not to be perfect and to make mistakes.

- Help them to embrace their differences. (This is what makes them unique.)

- Push them to be their best selves even when they don't think they are.

- Celebrate the good and the bad. (They need to be motivated even when they may not do their best.) It's okay!

- Do not make comparisons between others (i.e., siblings, classmates, or friends).

- Tell them they are smart and beautiful. (Speak life into them.)

The list above is only a source to assist you in helping your teens with positive self-esteem. Remember, we all play a part in how teens view society. We may not agree with all we see on social media or how they dress or talk, but at the end of the day, they matter, and what we say and do can and will affect them in a positive or negative way. As adults, it is our responsibility to shape and mold them for the better. Communicate openly with them and teach them to hold true to who they are; I promise they will not depart.

The poem at the beginning of this chapter by Patricia A. Fleming[2] is perfect because I, too, am on a personal quest to be my best version of myself. But I make sure to help the young people I encounter daily know they don't have to be perfect; in the end, they just have to be themselves.

~Peace & Blessing, always remember to Eat, Pray & Love

Ms. Janiqua LaChe'a

---

2 Patricia A. Fleming "My Personal Quest" (March 2018).

Dr. Adrian M. Woods Bio

Adrian M. Woods, EdD, is a writer, poet, counselor, veteran, and educator. He holds five collegiate degrees, including a master's and doctorate in education from the University of Houston Clearlake. He also holds a certification in counseling and mediation. Even with his credentials, he considers being a husband and father his greatest success. He uses his amazing and tragic experiences to explore and articulate life mysteries to help others navigate through their own trials and tribulations.

CHAPTER 2

Teens And Violence

By

Dr. Adrian Woods

———⚜——

With over fifteen years of experience in education, my memories are inundated with the faces of the countless students I have crossed paths with. Remembering every name and experience would be a daunting task for someone with an eidetic memory, so I will not even try. Despite this, there are certain students who forever will be etched on my heart. One of these students was a young man named Ruben. When someone looked at him, they most likely dismissed him as another Latin thug from the streets of Houston, Texas. Ruben was quiet and kept to himself. He carried himself like a "tough guy" and tried really hard to act the part. This often led to incidences of defiance, and that is what brought him into my office.

I was working as a behavioral interventionist at the time, and I spent most of my time mentoring those students who did not wish to attend school. At first, Rubin refused to even communicate with me, but my specialty has always been to relate to students caught in the street mentality. After weeks of feeling each other out and a trip to his house to encourage his attendance, Rubin finally began to open up to me. We would discuss what it was like growing up in a single-parent household, how living in Houston was different from when I was growing up, or how to get his grades up to attend shop class. Rubin turned out to be a very emotional and shy kid. He just felt he could not be himself and walk around his neighborhood safely. The last time I saw Rubin was the Friday before Thanksgiving break. He told me he was excited about hanging out with his girlfriend all break and eating. My departing words to him were, "You just be careful and get back here."

I'll never forget those words. Rubin died from gang violence during the break.

Teen violence is more than a fight on the basketball court. Teen violence ranges from bullying to sexual assault to homicide. On average worldwide, there are two hundred thousand homicides a year caused by teen violence. That is equivalent to 42 percent of the world's homicides being perpetrated by mere teenagers. This number is small compared to the number of teen injuries that require hospital treatment. In the United States in 2019, 126,130 juveniles were in the juvenile justice system for assaulting another person. This number does not include the 27,070 that were incarcerated for aggravated assault. Aggravated assault consists of any violent act that causes bodily injury or is performed with a deadly weapon. This does not also include the 3,000 incarcerated for attacking a family member, 120,000 incarcerated for destroying property, or the 44,000 institutionalized for numerous other violent crimes.

There is an old phrase, "Hurt people, hurt people." You may need to read that twice. This statement means that those who have inner turmoil tend to lash out at others. This could be family members or strangers on the street. Studies show one-third of those abused as children are likely to be abusers. And even though studies are unclear, the connection between children who have been victims of violence and those who commit violence has been documented by many researchers.

We think of teenagers as mini-adults. They are often tasked with responsibilities above their comprehension. This is an unfortunate piece of our modern society. In the 1940s, more women were forced to go out into the world to earn a living as their men marched off to WWII. This left the children to pick up the slack around the house with chores and even childcare. This is especially true for those from a low-economic or single-parent home. This led to the creation of the term *latchkey kid*. A latchkey kid is a child who is left at home while their guardians are at work. Approximately 1.4 million children in the US between the ages of eight and eighteen are responsible for caring for their siblings or younger adults. Younger kids who are left home alone face loneliness, boredom, and fear, while teenagers tend to be susceptible to peer pressure that potentially manifests in such behaviors as alcohol abuse, drug abuse, sexual promiscuity, and smoking, vandalism, and violence.

Does this mean that if you leave your children at home by themselves, they will become a murderer? Of course not. Is there a 100 percent answer to all the issues? No, but the information does show that our modern society's structure is prone to such behaviors. So do parents have a chance? We need to work. I cannot provide all the answers, but with nearly twenty years in educating and close to thirty years in raising kids in one way or another and being a violent teen, here are four steps I have utilized to assist in preventing, combating, and dealing with teens who are immersed in violent behavior.

Boundaries

Despite some modern trends, a teenager does not want to be your best friend. One of the best compliments a student ever gave me was, "Dr. Woods is cool, but he doesn't play that." In adult terms, that meant that I understood their situations and thought processes, but I would not let them act outside the rules or boundaries. Parents who allow their children to run the streets without any rules or consequences are not seen as the cool parents. They are the parents who do not care. I have heard from students of all genders and races that, "My parents aren't going to care." Or, "They don't punish me anyway." These students would prefer that their parents set boundaries; at least they'd know they cared.

This does not mean go home to your teenager and lay down the law. If you have not set a structure for discipline in your house, you will have a rebellious, angry teenager on your hands. Do not allow your child to speak to you in a certain manner. As soon as you allow one curse word, they will start cursing all through your house. As soon as you allow a child to push you, the next step is hitting you. I did not allow my child to hit me as an infant. Even someone that young is learning. This will set up the foundation for the future. When dealing with a teenager, you must set a line that must not be crossed. When you say stop, it stops. No haggling or negotiating. You are the parent. You are the authority in your house. If you do not set the boundaries at home, your child will not respect the boundaries of school or the road or know how to set boundaries for themselves.

Rules

Rules are different than boundaries. Boundaries are intrinsic, and rules are extrinsic. Rules are the physical manifestation of your boundaries. These are also the boundaries that you, as the parent, set for them, as the child. Rules are as important and as necessary as boundaries. Boundaries let them know to respect you and your house. Rules let them know that you plan to enforce those boundaries.

A parent must lay down the foundation from the beginning of a new activity. If a child receives a new video game system and you do not want them online all day, every day, you must set the boundaries. And do not have thirty-five rules and think they will be followed. Those rules will be forgotten as soon as they open the package. The rules also must be simple. My own boys cannot remember to clean their ears, so I know they will not remember something they do not want to do. Have about four rules that are specific because we all know teenagers are professional loophole finders. Examples of rules for the video game system are:

- No playing during the school week.

- No playing video games rated MA (mature audiences).

- All games off by 10:00 p.m.

- No arguing over the game.

Consequences

Boundaries mean nothing without consequences. Why do people follow laws? Please do not say it's because it's the right thing to do. People follow laws because they do not want to face the consequences. Nobody wants to have their day interrupted. You do not want to be inconvenienced. Neither does a teenager. There is not one consequence that supersedes another. A teenager will actually tell you what the consequence will be. My kids live on their cell phones. That is the first item I take away from them. Like I said, no one wants to be inconvenienced. You may ask, "What if they will not give me the cell phone?" Remember that you are the parent. You are the dominant force in your household. I am not telling you to beat down your child and snatch the cell phone if that's not your thing. You can turn off the phone with the provider and change the Wi-Fi password. Then while they are at school, take their power cords to their favorite electronic device.

Lastly, when it comes to the topic of consequences, do not threaten your child. If you say you are going to take the device, take the device. There is no other chance. The rule you do not enforce becomes the new rule, meaning that when you say you are going to give them another chance, that becomes the new rule, and the child knows they can push you to another level.

Listen and Talk

I placed this one last because this one can be difficult for new and old parents alike. Gone are the "ask your father" and "because I said so" days. Teenagers are smart, knowledgeable, and tech-savvy. I remember when growing up, if I asked "Why?" at any moment, my momma would slap all the taste out of my mouth and say, "Because I said so!" That had to be the end. She was my primary source of information. There was not a computer to check out the truth in history or to learn about a subject. I had to take her word for it. In 2022, children have information literally in the palm of their hands. Most of the time they have already researched a topic before they even ask you about the subject. Especially teenagers—they've asked their friends, watched a documentary on Netflix about it, and Googled it.

However, teenagers are still looking for validation and security. As a parent, listen to their feelings and thoughts. Sometimes you will listen and know it is foolishness before the sentence leaves their lips. That does not matter. The feeling they will receive because you just listened is invaluable. They will feel cared about and understood. Validate their ideas. An "I understand where you're coming from" works wonders. Then you can respond and correct them if necessary. I love to tell my three boys information about a subject and tell them to go Google it if they do not believe me. They roll their eyes but know I listen, respect them, and am willing to share my wisdom. And guess what? I admit when I am wrong. My mother still to this day, hates to admit she was wrong. Saying you are wrong makes it okay to make mistakes. Then you can show them that an adult fixes mistakes and does not hide them or let them fester. The simple act of listening and engaging your teenager in conversation works wonders.

There is no quick fix, and I could write a book on just the topics in this chapter. A violent teen is a complex personal matter. One last piece of advice I would suggest is to seek help if necessary. That could be with the school, a therapist, or the police. No one should be a victim of violence. The topics included in this chapter will make the transition easier.

References

Del Pozzo, Jill, et al. "The Influence of Childhood Trauma on Aggression and Violent Behavior in First Episode Psychosis: A Critical Review," 18 Oct. 2021, https://en.x-mol.com/paper/article/1450569150347771904.

Goleman, Daniel. "Sad Legacy of Abuse: The Search for Remedies." *The New York Times*, *The New York Times*, 24 Jan. 1989, https://www.nytimes.com/1989/01/24/science/sad-legacy-of-abuse-the-search-for-remedies.html.

Justice, National Center for Juvenile. "Estimated Number of Juvenile Arrests, 2019," https://www.ojjdp.gov/ojstatbb/crime/qa05101.asp.

"Young Caregivers." American Psychological Association, American Psychological Association, https://www.apa.org/pi/about/publications/caregivers/practice-settings/intervention/young-caregivers.

"Youth Violence." World Health Organization, World Health Organization, https://www.who.int/news-room/fact-sheets/detail/youth-violence.

Gracia Collins Rich Bio

Gracia is a seven-time bestselling author and editor. Her debut thriller, *Handkerchief*, reached #1 on Amazon's Bestsellers list in September 2020. Her writing expertise began with poetry and evolved into short stories, devotionals, and romance. She creates strong, relatable female characters with an edge and endings that are entirely unexpected. Gracia is also a coauthor of the *Glambitous! Guide to Winning in 2020* and the bestselling anthologies *Letters to Our Daughters* and *The Price for Greatness*

She is a featured writer and contributing editor at *Formidable Woman Magazine* and *WOE (Women Own Excellence) Magazine* and a featured writer for *Creating Your Seat at the Table Magazine*. Gracia has been featured on IHearThatGirl.com, SwagHer.com, Sheenmagazine.com, Glambitous! Magazine, Courageous Woman Magazine, and MizCEO Magazine.

Gracia is from Rains, South Carolina. She is the mother of four wonderful adult children and is a civil litigation and criminal defense paralegal.

CHAPTER 3

Teens And Parental Communication

By
Gracia Collins Rich

———— ❦ ————

How many times have you heard the phrase, "Parents just don't understand," even before Will Smith and DJ Jazzy Jeff turned it into a #1 hit? How often have you found yourself being the parent who didn't understand? If you have children, the times have been many. If your children are teens, then it's all the time. Most parents tend to forget when we were teens and suffered the same scenarios with our parents. We sometimes felt as though they didn't hear us, they didn't understand us, and it was their goal to undermine what we had going on. We thought they were know-it-alls and control freaks.

Now fast-forward a couple of decades, and *you* are the parent of teenagers. Hormone-raging, opinionated teens who feel it is their destiny to follow their dreams and heart's desires with no interference from you. That's right. NONE WHATSOEVER! So, what do you do? You try talking to them, but it never seems quite enough. Then you move on to threats to see your will be done, but the kids know that they are mostly idle, so they pay you no mind. It seems to you that nothing you say makes a real difference. There's no real connection. You begin to feel that teenagers are just going to have to figure it out themselves, or worse, the hard way. And sadly, this is where many parents give up. I don't know how many times I've heard family members say, "I can't talk to him or her. They don't listen. I give up."

Giving up is the worst thing you can do. In this chapter, it is my goal to give you some insight and tips on how to communicate with your teens. As a mother of both genders whose children are now young adults, I have had the distinct pleasure of learning how to communicate with my four children in ways that still work today. I have one daughter and three sons. All of them have different personalities and different communication styles. With that being said, one thing to always remember is that no two people are alike. It doesn't matter that they are all your children. It doesn't matter that they've all been raised the same way or that they are all the same gender. They are individuals, and the personalized approach is always best.

Do As I Say . . . Or Not!

Have you ever felt that you have had to force your teen into some understanding? We all have. We've told our teens to do something, and they haven't. We've told them to be on time, and they were late. We've told them to take out the trash only to find it still inside the next morning. And then we yell. We fuss. We get beside ourselves because we can't get them to do what we want. Once a conversation is had, sometimes our teens let us know that they do things or do not do things as we do. We provide examples, and they follow them, or so they say when it suits them. As parents, our general thought is, "Do as I say, not as I do." Let me be the first to let you know that this statement does not make a teen move faster. If anything, you may get a slow walk out of the room accompanied by a secret eye roll.

We as parents need to rethink the ways that we talk to our children, especially our teens. The way we communicate with them teaches them not only the way to communicate with others but also a sense of value in themselves. We should never talk down to them. We should speak to them in the same manner of respect that we speak to other adults. As a parent, we often think of our child as a person who is OURS. Ours in the sense of family. Ours as an extension of ourselves, but we don't treat them as such. We think of them as forever needing our guidance in all things. And sadly, we stifle ourselves. Teens are going through so much these days. In these times of social media frenzy, body shaming, racial tension, and parental expectations, they have a lot on their plates. Add to that hormonal and body changes, and we have a child in the midst of a life-changing event, going from childhood to adulthood.

This is the season when the way you communicate with your child will always be remembered. Were you too hard on them? Overly aggressive? Or did you listen, I mean really listen to see what was going on with them? One of the greatest communication skills is active listening. It's also one that parents lack the most. We tend to want to get our point across so that our teens will conform to what we want. We hear, but we don't listen. We overtalk and overanalyze and, in doing so, often miss out on what was really important to them. I'll be the first to say that this has been me. I have been so hell-bent at times on trying to get my point across to my teens that I missed the entire conversation. But once I realized that, I wasn't too adult to go back and talk with my teen. I wasn't embarrassed to say I was wrong. Another quick communication and life tip: Don't be afraid to say you were wrong. Our teens need to know that we are human. We make mistakes. We are not perfect. And believe it or not, your teen knows that. So the posturing is just for you.

Talking to your teen is one of the most valuable things you can do. It helps you both. I have learned so much from each of my children in their teen years that I could never write it all in this chapter. Their view of the world is so different from ours. They have bigger dreams than ours. They take things more seriously than some of us. They have their eyes on a future that we may never see. And how could we ever know that if we never spend the time talking to them? When I say talking, I don't mean that you have to schedule "talks" with your teen. I mean, you can, especially for things that are very important that require their full attention. But I'm talking more about casual but meaningful conversation. (We'll talk more about that in the upcoming pages.) It never has to be super serious. My teens have always been open with their communication with me. I know that is because I fostered that when they were very little. They could always come and talk to me, even if it wasn't about anything. I was always available to them. This made them feel safe and know that I was a trusting, nonjudgmental ear. Now let me be clear: I'm still the parent here, but I developed a system where my teens could talk to me about their issues, and we would work out a solution as a team instead of me always demanding that they do it my way. This system, however, doesn't always work, but I would always willingly give it a try.

Sugar & Spice . . . but *Not* Always Nice

Communication styles should be personalized, as I stated earlier in this chapter. Gender may not play an important role for many parents when it comes to communicating with their teens. However, it did and still does play an important role for me. My oldest child is female, and going from girl to woman was a trying time for us both. (LOL!) When you have a teen girl, there is so much going on with her and with you, for that matter. My communication style with my daughter evolved over the years. When she was a little girl, she was very similar to me, or the me I remembered from my childhood. She was studious and steadfast. She loved books and bossing her brothers around. She was easygoing and sweet. She never really questioned anything, and communicating with her was a breeze.

Enter the teen years! When my daughter became a teen, I felt that she was a terror. She was fierce, bold, opinionated, and questioned everything, and I mean *everything*! Our communication became a battle of extremes. It went from screaming matches to complete silence. We were either having a hot debate in which she knew she was right, or we weren't talking at all because we were angry. It has always been said, at least in my family, that girls typically don't get along with their mothers in their teenage years, that the female/female dynamic is a lot. I never wanted to believe that because I knew so many women who had excellent relationships with their mothers. I, on the other hand, was not one of those, so I was very concerned about my daughter, and I have a better one.

The thing that was causing the communication rift between my daughter and me was the fact that I wanted her to do what I wanted, and she was very much "herself" as a teen. She was always a person who has known herself, and I couldn't deal with that, so we had a tendency to clash. My daughter is also a very honest person who has no problem giving you the unvarnished truth. That was another thing I took exception to, especially coming from a teenager. Because I couldn't accept who my daughter was and was becoming, our communication suffered.

It took well into her older teen years before we could really talk to each other in a way that was understood and enjoyable. This actually came from doing things that were nonverbal. My daughter and I love many of the same things: books, movies, makeup, perfume, clothes, and food, to name a few. So one of our greatest forms of nonverbal communication was hanging out together on the weekend and going to our favorite places. We would go shopping and out to eat. During this time, we would talk about many things, both frivolous and serious. During these outings, we got to know each other a whole lot better. It is an actual situation of the nonverbal turning into verbal.

Bonding experiences can be a great way to usher in communication with your teen. Especially if it is something that *they* are interested in. Fortunately for me, my teens and I share many interests, so it's easier to create these moments. I think that as parents, we sometimes get hung up on the idea of *how* we should communicate with our teens instead of *what* we need to tell them. All information can be given in a variety of ways. That goes for feelings and emotions as well. We tend to turn communicating with our teens into a chore when it is really quite simple. My daughter and I are the best of friends now, talking daily about any and everything under the sun. This would not have been possible if I had never taken the time to get to know what communication type worked best for our relationship.

Frogs & Snails . . . and Definitely Male

My remaining three children are male. Being a mom to teenage boys is an incredible and exciting experience, but the communication setup is very different. My sons and I have always had the same open communication my daughter and I have, but I noticed that as my boys got older, they began to shy away from sharing everything with their mother. Their father became more so their go-to guy when they were in their early teens. He was the person who could relate to them for various reasons; the first one, most obviously, was the fact that he had been a teenage boy once himself. His approach to communication with the boys had more of a "life lesson talk" vibe. He would listen and then give advice based on the information provided and his life experiences. This was great for my sons' development into adulthood because I could teach them much, but I could not teach them how to be a man. I only offered advice if asked or gave a few pointers on anything they shared with me. I never came back and took a different stance than their father. We were united in the fact that this was the best way to communicate with the boys.

Then came the mid to late teens. When my sons got older and wanted to share different things about their lives with me, we normally did something together, much as I did with their sister. We would communicate and bond over video games (which I love) or comics and sometimes over funny stories told about their dating and college experiences. This allowed them to be open with me without it feeling "weird." This was the time when frustrations were let out and questions were asked. It was when I could find out if something was going on with them that needed addressing or if they just needed a hug from mom.

Teenagers aren't looking for us to go easy on them. We're parents. They know that we are responsible for them and their well-being. But despite what you may believe, your teen actually wants to talk to you. They want to know what you think of them. They want to know how you feel, and they want you to see who they are, not always through your eyes but with your ears and into your hearts. Our words can be our greatest asset or greatest curse when it comes to our children because they live on long after we're gone.

What Can Be Taught

When it comes to communication, we as parents can teach our teens many things. We can teach them how to use their words to introduce themselves to the world. We can teach them how to communicate with other people and that words have value. It is our place to show them the correct ways to communicate, how to get your message across without offense. We must teach our teens that everything that they are feeling is valid and can be expressed—in the right way. Communication is a powerful skill set. It is something talked about in interviews every day. Be it the way we speak, write, or send emails, the road to each and every relationship we will ever have, both personal and professional, begins with how well or how badly we communicate. We can teach our teens to master this art once we've mastered it ourselves.

What Can Be Learned

As an adult, we never give much thought to what we can learn from our teenagers, especially on subjects that we think we know everything about. We would never believe that someone so young could school us in something we've been doing for decades. If that's your thought, I'll be the first to tell you that you're wrong. We all have been wrong when it comes to what can be learned from our teens. My teenagers taught me that all communication isn't lip service. Everything doesn't need a long monologue from me to be understood. They taught me that when they speak, it is essential, and if I'm trying so hard to show my authority, I will miss something. They have taught me that words are not always needed. So much can be shared from parent to child through a look, a reassuring gesture, and a bit of free time laughing with each other. It's not as nearly as hard as we would believe, nor is it as easy as we think. There is a nuance to it, a sweet spot right there in the middle where a door opens, leading both sides to peace and understanding. When you reach it, you and your teen will have the best communication of your lives.

Gregory L. Bloomfield Bio

I was born in Toronto, Canada, to a West Indian family. My parents are both from the beautiful island of Jamaica. I am everything I am because of my West Indian and Canadian upbringing. I currently reside south of Boston, Massachusetts.

As a professional, I am an accountant and a licensed CPA in the state of Massachusetts. However, my real passion is in ministry, as I am a preacher and speaker to youth, young adults, and particularly men. My ministry has taken me all across New England, New York, Florida, and Canada.

I serve as an elder and as the men's ministry director for the Attleboro Seventh-Day Adventist church under the leadership of pastor Luis Peguero. I am also an amateur musician, as I play the saxophone and dabble with the flute, piano, and drums.

My greatest pride and joy is being a single father of two teenagers, Thaddeus, fifteen, and Isabelle, thirteen.

I am fairly new to the writing space, but with DFG, it has been a great experience, and I look forward to writing more books in the future. Most importantly, I love Christ, and I am a living testimony of how God can restore someone's life from the guttermost to the uttermost.

CHAPTER 4

Teens And Divorce

By

Gregory L. Bloomfield

Introduction

It should be no surprise to anyone when I make this
statement. When it comes to marriage and the family,
divorce has become a dubious norm, particularly in North
American society. In fact, it has changed the way we define
family and parenting, especially from the perspective of
teenagers. One teenager's reality may be that their mother and
father both live at home, possibly with other siblings from the
same parents. Another teenager's reality could be that they
just live with their mother because Mom and the teenager's
father had a divorce, and Dad doesn't come around much, but
his biweekly child support check does. Another teenager's
reality is that they live with their father and his new wife and
her two kids, what we would call the *blended family*. All of this

has become a reality for so many, and the family is not a one-size-fits-all definition anymore.

Consider the following statistics regarding marriage and divorce and how they can affect children[3]:

- The US has the world's highest rate (23 percent) of children living in single-parent households.

- Twenty-four million children in the United States live with an unmarried parent.

- 65 percent of children in the US lived with two married parents in 2017. **Only 65 percent.**

- In 2018, about 780,000 divorces took place in the United States.

- 76 percent of Americans think getting a divorce is morally acceptable.

---

3 Mrkonjic, Elma "19+ Children of Divorce Statistics That Will Make You Cry," The High Court (web blog), 12 October 2021, https://thehighcourt.co/children-of-divorce-statistics/.

- Divorce and children statistics show that one-in-five children born in wedlock will experience a parental breakup by the age of nine.

- According to children of divorce statistics, 31 percent of children younger than six have experienced a change in their family or household structure.

- Child custody stats show that 4.64 million single parents in the US had custody and received child support in 2011.

- In 2014, there were more than 13.4 million parents separated from their child's other parent.

And this is the most salient point that the statistics show, and thus the point of this chapter:

A University College London study examined the effects of divorce on children's behavior. The findings revealed that children whose parents divorced when they were **between the age of seven and fourteen** are considerably more likely to experience behavioral and emotional issues. The divorced parents' effect on a child results in a worrying **16 percent increase in such problems**.[4]

The purpose of this chapter is to give some ways to navigate through the journey of divorced parenting with your child, particularly if your child is a teenager.

Before I begin, I must tell you that I am an accountant and not a child psychologist or therapist. So you are probably asking what in the world would qualify me to speak on such a topic. I am so glad you asked. The reason I can speak on this subject with some authority is because I LIVED IT! I have been through the painful process of divorce with children, and I don't wish this on my worst enemy. Divorce is like death, and the only difference is that you can't bury your ex-spouse; he or she will keep on living, and you have to find ways to communicate with him or her because you created lives together . . . your children. I was divorced in 2012 when my son, Thaddeus, was five and my daughter, Isabelle, was three. Many of the things I am going to mention in this chapter are

---

4 Mrkonjic, Elma "19+ Children of Divorce Statistics That Will Make You Cry," The High Court (web blog), 12 October 2021, https://thehighcourt.co/children-of-divorce-statistics/.

from my personal journey, along with some missteps along the way. Today, and at the time of this chapter, I am a single father of two teenagers; Thaddeus is fifteen, and Isabelle is thirteen; we have a great relationship, but it took a lot of work and prayer. I would like to share my journey with you, and hopefully, it can inspire you to know that divorce is horrible, but you can still be an amazing parent to your teenagers and hopefully have a wonderful coparenting relationship with your ex-spouse.

Help Yourself First

I am originally from Toronto, Canada, and currently live outside of Boston, Massachusetts. My mother, two brothers, most of my family, and my childhood friends are still in Toronto. I wanted to take my children to visit their grandmother for Canadian Thanksgiving, which is the same time as Indigenous Peoples' Day in October. The kids and I would usually drive to Toronto, which is about an eight-to-ten--hour drive depending on how long we had to wait at the Canadian/US Border. This time, I wanted to take the kids on a plane, which would be only an hour's flight from Boston to

Toronto. I think my kids were eight and six years old at the time. We went to the airport, checked in our bags, went through security, sat down, and waited to board the plane. When we finally got to our seats, we heard the instructions from the pilot and the stewardesses on the plane. There was one particular instruction that stuck in my mind, and it involved the oxygen masks. The stewardess demonstrated how to put on the masks in case there was cabin pressure. She said that the flow of oxygen would come into the mask, and we had to tightly secure the mask behind our heads and breathe in and out of the mask. Does that sound familiar to you if you are a frequent air traveler? Well, the salient point is this: the stewardess said, "You need to secure your mask first before you try to help others." In other words, I had to make sure that I was breathing properly before I could help my own children. This seems counterintuitive in this culture, but there's actually a lot of wisdom in this when we are dealing with parenting and divorce.

When you are a divorced parent of teenagers, it is critical that you take care of yourself and that you are a healthy individual before you can properly raise your children. In fact, you must take care of yourself before you can contribute to any facet of society, whether it is your job, your friends, your family, your new relationship, or your community at large. You must take care of your mental, emotional, physical, and spiritual health first. How do you do that? Well, I am a huge proponent of mental and emotional health therapy. There are therapists and counselors out there that deal specifically with divorce. Why? Divorce is like death. It is the death of a dream, and with any death of a family member or a friend, there is trauma. If you haven't already dealt with this death and trauma, I urge you to find a therapist in your area and go through the divorce recovery steps. Someone introduced me to a divorce recovery therapist, and I participated in a twelve-week course. It was difficult, and it was painful, but I don't believe that I would be the parent I am today without it. Once you have the mental health resources in your corner, then you will have the tools to properly care for your children, just like putting on their masks on the plane after you put on yours.

I would also encourage therapy for your teenagers so they can express their feelings about the divorce and so your family has strategies to deal with this "new normal" and help avoid the 16 percent increase in behavioral and emotional problems.

Along with mental and emotional health, a divorced parent should practice a good diet, exercise, and sleep. I would also encourage taking spiritual health into consideration. As for me, I am a Christian, and attending church along with service to others truly helps me. You can do the same in your place of worship, and if you are not a believer in anything, you can turn to nature, hobbies, and other activities that holistically help you so that you can be better for your teenagers. Please make sure that you put on your oxygen mask before you try to help your children with theirs.

Extra Love

Oftentimes people feel that teenagers do not need us as much. After all, they can feed themselves (as long as you provide the food), take their own showers, make their own beds, and wake up on their own. They probably have a lot of friends, so they do not even talk to you as much as they do their friends. My children will text me more than they call me when they are at their mother's house, and when they text me, it is usually because they need money.

But to be serious, do not ever think that your teenagers do not need you. In fact, I would like to declare that at the teenage stage, they need more love and guidance than ever before. I remember when I was a teenager, and probably a preteen, I had a lot of questions as to why my life was the way it was. My parents split up when I was three, and there were times I thought I may have been the reason why. Deep down, I knew that this was not true, but frequently I thought about it. I would like to believe that most children blame themselves for their parents' breakup. It is your role as a divorced parent to a teenager, whether your teenager lives with you or not, to reinforce your love for them and your commitment to their happiness.

Maybe you have heard the saying that love is an action word. You may have also heard that love is a verb and not a noun. When one loves someone, they commit their time to them, and they are willing to freely give to that person. If you want to show your love to your children, then you can tell them that you love them, but always *show* them that you love them. How? Well, here is an example from my own life. Per my parenting agreement, I have my children every other weekend. No matter what is going on during my life, I am committed to my children, and I pick them up on Friday evenings and drop them off with their mother on Sunday evenings. The first step to showing love is consistency and then showing up. When I have them, my job does not matter; my hobbies do not matter; time with them matters. I make that time special and let them know that I love them, and we do many things together, such as reading, cooking, homework, watching movies, going to church, visiting other friends, and sometimes, just doing nothing but being in each other's presence. Let us keep in mind that I am not just a parent every other weekend but every day, so I keep the communication open anytime during the week. That means phone calls, surprise visits, text messages, and other creative ways for each of my teenagers to feel secure in their father's love.

Loving my children also includes being fiscally responsible. Now, you may think that this is solely paying child support. I would like to challenge you to think outside of the box and know that teenagers need so much more. As their father, I have to plan for the future, which includes a college fund, a savings account for them when they become older, and also teaching them about finances so they can be independent when they are older and not just depend on Daddy for everything.

Loving my children is saying yes sometimes, saying no sometimes, and never being indifferent. Loving my children is also allowing my teenagers to love and honor their mother. Regardless of what happened between us, that is not their worry or their concern. My teenagers have a right to love us both equally and without the feeling of divided loyalties. They should never feel guilty that they are loving their father and neglecting their mother or vice versa. It is these stresses that cause kids to have emotional and behavioral problems in school, at church, and in the world.

One of my mentors told me that I am contributing to my teenagers' ability to have healthy relationships with other human beings by the way I show love to them. My son is going to be someone's father, someone's husband, and someone's boyfriend. My daughter is going to be someone's mother, someone's wife, and someone's girlfriend. Therefore, showing extra love and care, not just in words but in daily actions, is the key to the divorced parent having success with their teenage children.

Stay Connected

As I mentioned in the previous section, love is an action and not just words. Therefore, loving your children means that you will stay connected to them. How? By making their lives a top priority in your life. After caring for your mental and emotional well-being, which is not a one-time event, you should care for your teenagers' mental and emotional well-being as well. It is imperative that you let your children know that they can tell you anything that is on their minds. Many teenagers feel that they cannot talk to their parents because they just do not get it. Or teenagers feel that their mother or father just is not cool. (I have heard that a few times, so do not feel bad.) I think that is because we try to preach to our teenagers and not listen to what they are saying. We as adults must understand that we were once teenagers and we thought that we knew everything. Give your teenagers grace, especially if you are a divorced parent.

Sometimes your teenagers may complain about the other parent, especially in a divorced situation. Never give your teenager the green light to bash the other parent—no matter if that other parent is dead wrong and truly is a jerk. When you bash the other parent of your teenager, you are setting up the seed for disrespect in the future against you. Trust me when I tell you this; nothing good will come out of that situation. Do not do it! I repeat, do not do it!

Staying connected also means knowing their schedule and what they are doing in their lives. Do you know your teenager's teachers? Do the teachers know you? What about their grades? Their extracurricular activities? Their likes? Their dislikes? People do not care what you know until they know that you care. Now, if that applies to grown adults, then you know it applies to your teenagers. Stay connected to them because it shows that you love them and care about their total well-being.

If Possible, Live Peaceably

As I stated earlier, I identify as a Christian, and one of my favorite passages in the Bible comes from Romans 12:18, which reads:

If it is possible, as much as depends on you, live peaceably with all men.[5]

It is important that you work toward peace with your ex-spouse so you can properly raise your teenager in unity so your teenager will not be part of the 16 percent that I mentioned earlier in this chapter. The verse mentions as much as it depends on you. Therefore, you have to find your oxygen mask first and breathe in peace and forgiveness for your ex-spouse, for your sake and for your teenager's sake.

You, as an adult, can and most likely will find love again with someone else, and guess what, so can your ex-spouse. However, your teenager, no matter how long ago the divorce was, will never have their mother and father together again. So who is the biggest beneficiary of peace? You guessed it!

---

5 Romans 12:18, New King James Version

Your children. Remember, you have had your childhood and your teenage years, but your children have not, so for no other reason, try to be peaceful with your ex-spouse.

That sounds good, but you don't know what they did to me! I understand. But I still urge you, for your teenager's sake—live peaceably. Now, I realize that some people do not know peace because there is no peace within them. I get it! Therefore, you have to protect your peace and set up healthy boundaries with your ex-spouse, which may mean that you do not get all of the information about your teenager. This is why I said, stay connected and make the time you have with your teenager precious. Children turn into teenagers, teenagers turn into young adults, and young adults turn into adults. This is only for a time. And when the time is up, you can have the relationship with your child that you always wanted; but it is important that you sow the seeds of peace now and live peace within yourself. You owe it to yourself and to your teenagers.

Hopefully, these nuggets of wisdom from my own experiences help you along the way of your journey. I wish you all the best in your parenting journey with your teenager(s). Divorce does not have to be the end, but it can be the start of a wonderful new beginning.

Shalom!

Shaundra Dineen Bio

Shaundra Dineen is a best-selling author, award-winning motivational speaker, podcast host, and founder of Rubyz Global Coaching and Consulting LLC. Armed with her relentless motivation and her inspiring commitment to empowering women of all backgrounds to dream big and triumph over adversity, Shaundra's authentic, dynamic speaking style has led her to become an internationally acclaimed speaker for conferences and corporate events. With her life-changing approach to personal development, she's on a mission to help women succeed in every stage of their lives—whether they're top-level business executives, corporate professionals, or college grads fresh out of school.

As the founder of the *Do It Afraid Podcast* and the coauthor of the hit faith-based book *Pray, Pursue, Persist: Testimonies of Women Who Soar Through the Power of Prayer*, Shaundra is passionate about energizing women to help them reach their full potential by taking charge, overcoming fear, and finding the courage to live their best lives. Shaundra's coaching skills have helped hundreds of women transform their situations and move from pain to power.

Shaundra lives by the mantra, "Do It Afraid," and she's determined to help other women live by it too. She enjoys spending time with her family and practicing her faith when not working. To learn more about Shaundra and her work, visit her website at www.lifecoachshaund.com or email info@lifecoachshaund.com.

CHAPTER 5

Teens And Pregnancy

By
Shaundra Williams

———————— ◆◆◆ ————————

act: In an article published by the Centers for Disease Control and Prevention, more than four out of five, or 80 percent, of teenage pregnancies are unintended.[6]

Fact: Teenage pregnancy is defined as pregnancies in girls under the age of twenty, regardless of marital status.

Fact: In 1991, there were 16.8 births per one thousand females under the age of twenty. The United States began to see a decline in teenage pregnancies from 1991 to 2009; however, within that eighteen-year span of time, 1991 was the highest year for teenage pregnancies.

Fact: I was one of the teenage moms included in these statistics.

---

6 "Vital Signs: Teen Pregnancy—United States 1991–2009" 2011.

My Truth

I was fifteen years old when I became pregnant. I remember the moment of conception like it was yesterday. It was a simple game of Truth or Dare. Spin the bottle; if the bottle lands on you, you decide rather you will answer a question with truth or accept a dare. Once you decide, there is no changing your mind.

My friends and I sat around in a circle; the bottle landed on one of the boys in the group. He chose to accept the dare instead of answering a question with truth. The dare was to ask a girl in the group to have sex with you. Now, I am pretty sure none of us even knew what it really meant to have sex with someone, but it sounded like a fair dare as he looked around the group and pointed at me. He chose me. At that moment, I was excited to be chosen. I was somewhat of an awkward teenager. I didn't have many friends outside of family. I lived a very sheltered life. I definitely did not have the "street smarts" of the other players in the game. In my mind, being chosen at that moment said to everyone else that I was cool just like they were.

It was now time to answer the dare. It was over summer break, and my mom was away at work, so we went into my bedroom. The day was Monday, August 20, 1990. I can recall the date because it was the day MC Hammer debuted on the *Oprah Winfrey Show*. I remember watching him dance across the screen in his sequined outfit, dancing with such intensity to "You Can't Touch This" that I was mesmerized. I wasn't paying attention to what was happening to my body. Past trauma had taught me to disengage in moments of fear or confusion. (We will revisit this later.) I chose to focus on MC Hammer instead of focusing on the moment. That moment, those five minutes changed my life forever.

At fifteen, I was not psychologically prepared for the new normal of my life. Because of my strict upbringing, I was isolated from my peers during this time. I was no longer treated like a fifteen-year-old girl. I was now a fifteen-year-old pregnant girl. I should have been experiencing a carefree, fun, adventurous life. Instead, I was adjusting to the changes in my body and trying to figure out how to handle this stage of my life. I remember thinking, "How did I get here? Where did I go wrong?" My family was a middle-class, two-income household with both parents present in the home. Both were staples in the community. They kept my brothers and me involved in church and other community activities. We were "good" kids. I was a "good" girl. Yet there I was, sitting in the doctor's office with my mother, preparing for an ultrasound.

My body was just as confused as my mind was. I continued to have monthly menstrual cycles until I was almost seven months pregnant. In fact, when I told the doctor this, he became concerned that I had possibly had a miscarriage and my body had aborted the fetus without me realizing what had happened. Little to no weight gain happened over the first seven months of the pregnancy. I could not recall feeling flutters or movement in my stomach. These were all alarming signs.

After many tests and multiple ultrasounds, it was determined that everything was okay with the baby. On April 28, 1991, I delivered a healthy seven-pound, eleven-ounce baby boy that changed my life forever. From that moment forward, I was no longer living only for myself. I was a mother living for both of us.

The Next Chapter

Fact: Teen pregnancy impacts many aspects of the teen mom that are often left undealt with. Although there has been a decrease in teen pregnancy over the last twenty years, there are still open triggers that can leave teen moms and their support system feeling unsupported and lost. For the teenage mom, there are social consequences, including stigma and feelings of rejection from parents, peers, and social groups. The long-term consequences include lower educational achievement, medical complications, higher subsequent fertility, low labor force participation, reduced earnings, a lifetime of economic stress and limited opportunity, and marital failure. The long-term effect on the infant includes an increased incidence of both mental subnormality and neurologic problems.[7]

Fact: When a teenager becomes pregnant, it is reasonable to expect that this affects the entire family dynamic. The baby often becomes part of the family household and requires a

---

7 A.G. Pecoraro, F.B. Robichaux, J.G. Theriot, Teen Pregnancy; Effect on Family Well Being, Spring 1987.

great deal of care and attention. With close to 80 percent of teens continuing to reside within the family of origin one year after they give birth[8] and with the younger siblings of teenage mothers themselves having an elevated rate of early parenthood,[9] such effects on the family surely have important practical implications.

After giving birth to my son, there were so many changes in my life and in the life of my family. We now had almost a fourth child. My son grew up in a community of love. He was provided for at every turn. However, I was left to try to pick up the pieces and keep my life together. How does a fifteen-year-old cope with the idea that she is now a mother? When most teenagers were enjoying high school athletics, birthday parties, concerts, and the freedom that comes with adolescence, I was managing high school, part-time employment, a babysitter, Pampers, formula, and all the other things necessary in raising a child. To this day, I can't explain how I did it, but I can explain a few things that I think carried

---

8 Hogan, Hao, & Parish, 1990; Trent & Harlan, 1994.

9 Cox, Means, & Bithoney, 1993; East & Felice, 1992; Friede et al., 1986

me through this new chapter of life: resilience, tenacity, and a drive to prove the statistics wrong. I was determined to be the one teenage mom that was not limited by the choice I made on August 20, 1990. I was determined to defy the odds and make myself and my family proud. I wanted to make up for the assumed burden I had brought to my family, the embarrassment, the added responsibility. I wanted to be the one that made it out.

There were two quotes that fueled this desire. One was from my mother in somewhat of a warning, but a message received, nonetheless. She said, "One time is a mistake. The second time is a choice." The next quote was from my best friend's mom. She said, "You can make it through this. You are not the sum of this moment in your life." Those two quotes, to this day, ring loudly in my soul. It was those two messages that motivated me to share my story with other teenage moms and their families. My message, mission, and goal are just as clear today as they were thirty-one years ago. My life's journey is about me, but it is to be shared so that others find hope and encouragement not to give up.

To any teenage mom that may pick up this book and read my story, I want to share with you the possibilities that are available for you if you make the decision not to be held hostage by the mistake of a moment. You are not the sum of the mistake. You are not a statistic. You are only what you believe you are. You have the ability to set the course your life will take moving forward. Consider this moment as a reset. The moment has happened, and now it's time to make the best of it. Take charge of your life. Be resilient, tenacious, and determined. I went on to graduate from high school with honors and attended Lamar University in Beaumont, Texas. I did this with my son in tow. I had to be a bit more strategic than others, but all that mattered was that I was obtaining the education that statistics said I would not be able to obtain. I married my college sweetheart and moved to the city of Houston, Texas, where I began working in the healthcare field. I worked my way up from being a medical assistant to becoming the practice manager for one of the most prestigious, sought-after orthopedic surgeons in the area. I understood the value of hard work and determination. I was so proud of myself. I had beat the odds. I had beat the statistics. However, this wasn't enough. I wanted to continue to beat the statistics. I wanted more for my life, and I wanted to help other teenage moms.

I stumbled into post-secondary education as a career coach for students that were in situations just as I had experienced— single moms who were trying to find their grip on life. Over the span of seventeen years, I went from working as a coordinator to becoming the first African-American vice president of workforce development for the largest post-secondary vocational trade school organization in the country—all because I had the tenacity, resilience, and desire to beat the odds. You read the statistics above. According to that, I should not have experienced the successes that I have. God was with me in 1990, and he has carried me all the way this far.

As for my son, he is a living reminder that anything is possible, and all of my life's journeys were necessary to get both of us to this point. It is ironic that I am writing this on the day that he turns thirty-one. The baby that went seven months with no prenatal care, that should have been born with Down syndrome, that we could barely find a heartbeat for during that first ultrasound, that had the odds stacked against him as the child of a teenage mom and double-stacked as an African American male that grew up without his father in his life, but had the most amazing father figures in my brothers and daddy—he is thriving. He is well. He is my heartbeat walking the earth. I would often look at him and pray that my mistakes did not negatively impact his life. I am sure many teen moms look at their children in the quiet moments and pray that they will make better choices than she has. I had those thoughts. I would often say to my son, "Do good for me because when I was your age, I was not doing so good." Even prior to pregnancy, I had experienced many challenges, which I learned as an adult could have impacted my decision-making skills. Sexual trauma leaves behind ugly scars that seek healing but do not know where to look. It was easy to shift my focus to the *Oprah Winfrey Show* that day because life to that point had taught me that allowing someone to take advantage of my body meant that I was accepted. I buried some of those scars but carried others into my adult life. It wasn't until I sought counseling that I learned that my decisions were not my own. They were how I thought I was supposed to live. My son is the best part of me. I am grateful for the healing and the journey he brought to my life.

To the family, friends, mentors, teachers, pastors, Sunday school teachers, aunts, uncles, peers, and anyone else who crosses a teen mom's path, It is not your job or responsibility to judge her. She has enough to carry without your stares and negative comments. She is carrying the consequence of her own mistake and the beauty of a new life. Show love. Extend grace. Forgive her and help her move on. Also, extend this same thing to her parents. They do not deserve to be judged by what they are experiencing.

My son and I are proof that good can come from mistakes. I want every other teen mom to experience the same. Know that you are loved.

Jason Williams Bio

Jason is a two-time Amazon bestselling author with DFG. He is a businessman with Miller Williams Financial Consulting LLC and a musician as the organizer of The Band, www.thebandwa.com. One of his goals in life is to leave everyone he connects with more enriched and enlightened.

CHAPTER 6

Teens And Spirituality

By
Jason Williams

———————— ⚜ ————————

This particular subject is near and dear to my heart, being raised in a household where my mother and father were very active in ministry and trying to navigate my growth into adulthood and figure out who I was personally as well as spiritually. Growing up in my household, church wasn't an option. If there was a service and my parents were going, we were there, no questions asked, and we were serving in some capacity. As teens, my brothers and I were young musicians groomed by our parents to serve in church, being that my father was a pastor. We were the music department. We were given instruments at early ages and were taught to play enough to carry a service, and any service, anywhere my parents went. So as I am sure you can tell, we were raised with the expectation of being in church, and not just being there, but working. But for us, it was hard growing up because we had to learn to have a dual life.

We had church friends who most times never knew our school friends. We had to be able to separate church life from out-of-church life. We had to learn to manage how we talked and interacted with our peers in different settings. We had to accept that our lives were different from a lot of our friends', and there was nothing we could do about it. There were things we had to miss and not be a part of because of something that, frankly, we had no choice in. Luckily for my brothers and me, we did not grow up with animosity for the church, but we do have some lingering effects of the choices made for us.

Now don't get me wrong, my parents did not keep us from playing sports or hanging out with our friends and enjoying our youth, but we had to create a lane in each world we lived in to fit in where we were. We had to develop skills that, at that age, we probably weren't ready for, but because of the demand of our parents, it caused us to mature unwillingly. We had to realize early that our life was to be in service to God, and to do so sometimes meant we couldn't do everything we wanted because ministry took precedence. We also learned that sometimes the service you rendered wasn't for you but for someone else you may never know. We weren't wholly unbalanced, but we were definitely God driven. That isn't a bad thing, and at that time, it kept us out of a lot of possible trouble from being idle.

I said all of that to say this, teens today are dealt a different set of cards, and life is a lot more complicated, but I believe that with the right approach, we can groom our teens to love life and God and keep it balanced. Today's teens have so much more information at their fingertips that they have to process, so trying to figure out who they are is now more convoluted than ever before, and adding the pressure of trying to figure out their spirituality is tougher than ever. Especially in the society in which we live, there are so many things pulling on the minds of our youth, such as gender issues, legal drugs, having sex, etc.

We as parents now must almost be clinical psychologists to handle the reality our children live in. We must walk sensitively in a society that says we can't say this or that without being labeled something negative because our opinions don't line up with the majority of the masses. Yet we still have to parent our children when they are hurting, rejected, or feeling lost, but stay politically correct so as to not offend them or their peers. Word choice is difficult when your children or their peers choose different pronouns. So just the idea of raising children alone is much more complicated than it was a decade or so ago. With all this at hand, how do you throw in the area of spirituality and make it all make sense? To be honest, I don't know! There are so many different religious beliefs and systems of understanding spirituality that even that is more complicated than it used to be. What I believe may not be what you believe, and I have to be okay with that because that's your choice. So with all of this, this chapter is very difficult to deliver all that needs to be conveyed, but I am going to do my best in trying to give some good points.

Do You Really Know Your Child?

I think a lot of us know our children on the surface, and for most, it's not a negative. We know them by how we have trained them to express themselves around us. You are their parent, and a lot of how we deal with our teenagers is "Do what I say," or was that just me? Have you created an avenue for them to truly feel comfortable having conversations that may be hard for them to have and you may not want to hear, but they can talk to you and feel safe to express their feelings and be heard? As the head of your household or as the parental figure, you may sense where you are is good because they speak about some things, but have you truly accepted the fact they may choose to talk to others about things they perceive you can't handle from them? Are you okay with letting them express themselves and not take it personally when it kind of hits home for you? Most times, as a parent, I had to learn that I have to give them room to grow into the individual I want them to be. But to do that, I also have to grow with them and see them as more than my child and more as an emerging adult. Now don't get me wrong, parenting most definitely comes first, but you have to make room for the transition that comes next so you don't lose them early and have to redevelop a new relationship.

This is the first step in getting your teen into accepting whatever spirituality you subscribe to. I know those that know me know what I believe, but for the sake of this book, I wanted to be more universal because it's about the young adults. Growing up, God was a central part of my life, and I was raised that way, but today some have no ties to religion, and if you want to win them, then they have to be tied to you so they hear you and understand that where you are coming from is a place of love and not dogma. If they feel you are truly concerned about them as an individual, then they are more receptive to your guidance and influence. I know some of you are saying, "How can my child feel as if I am not concerned about them with all I do for them?" A lot of us as parents are busy taking care of them and not wholeheartedly involved in what they are into. We are going to games and events, but are we really sitting down and building a level of influence to where you are the biggest influencer in their life?

I understand that when our children reach the teen years, we are trying to keep them from making serious mistakes, and we should, but we also have to be able to steer them with influence and not just strength.

Are You Sure about What You Believe?

I say this with the utmost humility. Do you clearly understand what you believe? Can you explain what you believe, or do you rely on others to teach your children what you say you believe? Most people like going to their place of worship, but when you go home, is what you say you believe exemplified in your home? I know I grew up with the, "Do what I say," mantra. However, my parents showed us what it was like to be involved in ministry, probably more than I would have preferred growing up, and when it came to spirituality, they didn't just say listen to me, but they also showed us by how they lived. Statistically, it has been shown that when the parents are involved in some sort of religious or spiritual habit, their children follow that pattern. Teens are very impressionable as they go through physical, hormonal, and mental changes. So it is very hard to get them to hear things from you and not take them the wrong way, but you can be the perfect example of what you believe, and they won't be able to refute the results.

I remember in the '80s on Long Island, there was a hurricane coming, and we fortified our house as best as we could. I remember, though, that my dad and mom made us come together and pray. As the storm was approaching our area, the skies were darkened, and we heard the winds picking up while we were praying, and then there was silence. When my father ended the prayer, we looked out the windows; the sun was shining, and no wind was blowing. We were told it was the eye of the storm, and this was going to be a short reprieve from the storm, but the storm never returned. It was clear for the rest of the day. I remember that distinctly because I was then introduced to the power of prayer that my parents always talked about but I had never really known for myself. I saw them put into action what they believed, and the result was astounding to the teen me. I will forever believe in the power of prayer, and no one can take that from me. My experience in that scenario is the same as you could have if you are consistent in what you believe.

And the opposite is the case for those that don't exemplify consistency. You teach your children that you don't really live what you say you believe, and they will not gravitate to it because, to them, it is fake because it appears to be fake to you.

Spirituality is an important piece to your child's life journey because it gives them something to lean on when there appears to be nothing else at times. Spirituality for your teen, as well as you, is the strength to keep pushing for something greater than just hasn't manifested. We all need some type of religion, spirituality, or whatever you choose to call it because without it, when times get hard, and they will, we need to be able to pull from the source that gives us life and strength to keep pushing. It also helps to govern the way we treat others and ensures there is some type of moral standard. It helps to build identity, and it helps to strengthen character. I believe that we are all connected by God and that we all need to be connected to God in action. The connection to God allows us to reap the full benefit of His resources. It is just like having multiple children at home. The one that seems to stick by you more seems to get more just from constantly being in the vicinity. It's not that others can't do the same. They choose not to. They may receive the basic benefits of being a part of the family, but that child that spends more time with Mom or Dad seems to accept more from Mom and Dad. It's not always the tangible things either. Sometimes it's the things that matter most, not the things that can be collected in a box or put on a shelf, but those things that you only get with time spent in their presence. Those are the things you should want for your children to have so they will be entirely supplied with all the tools needed not just to survive but also to thrive. Spirituality helps us have a more hopeful outlook on life. It helps some people to have a sense of community or brotherhood. It helps to create a bond with others of like mind, and it helps to create a support group organically, with a sense of being connected to something bigger. Don't be afraid or feel like you are controlling if you decide to direct your children toward some sort of spirituality; it only makes them better and stronger.

Leatrice Lindsay Bio

Leatrice Lindsay is a serial entrepreneur, health and wellness coach, wealth builder, healer, and speaker. Her gifts are centered on helping women experiencing burnout or recovering from burnout to realign and bring harmony to their mind, body, and spirit through holistic transformation and proven self-mastery technique ~ I AM Becoming!

CHAPTER 7

Teens And No Parents

By
Leatrice L. Lindsay

———————

I am loved . . . Before I dive in, I want you to know, you are loved.
Before I formed you in the womb, I knew you before you were born,
I set you apart: I appointed you as a prophet to the nation.

(Jerimiah 1:5)

How beautiful is it to know that you are loved, beloved? One of the things we often struggle with as teenagers is our identity. This is the time we feel and see life's changes happening right in front of our eyes as we enter what seems like a new world called high school. This is the time you get asked, "Who are you?" and are expected to know where you will be in the next five to ten years. Another question is what college/university you will attend and so on. As important as these questions are, they could add to the confusion and doubts a teen or an adopted child may have during this cycle of their life.

Allow me to share my story with you. Ever since I can remember, my mother has always extended herself to others. There was always room for guests. And we had many. By the time I got to high school, I remember her going as far as taking the required classes to become a certified foster mom. As a teen, I wanted my parents' attention and loved my space, so the thought of sharing any of those did not rub me so well. I was all in my feelings.

In later years, after all the amazing connections I made with each encounter, I started looking forward to a new bonus brother or sister, aunt, or uncle and developed great relationships with awesome individuals I would have never had the opportunity to meet had my mother not opened her heart and home.

Many adolescents experience these same emotions. An adolescent living without their parents is no different. I was often the ear for many of my bonus brothers and sisters, a trusted source of communication, bonding together while finding comfort in an unfamiliar place.

The missing pieces to the puzzle will always be a void with unanswered questions until you can sit and feed your soul. Here are a few examples of emotions and behaviors I recognized in all teens, not only those who may have feelings of abandonment. These are commonalities we all have as we journey to independence and adulthood. Rest assured, you are not alone. If you can identify one or more that stands out for you, write them down and start to fill your cup.

1. Self-esteem – Searching self to identify who you are becoming

2. Personal confidence or lack of it

3. Identity

4. Seeking validation

5. Trust issues

6. Codependence

7. Emotional issues

8. Sexual temptation

9. Peer Pressure

10. Feeling of rejection

The Battlefield of Our Mind

You are becoming, and every day you have the opportunity to create who you will become. —Leatrice Lindsay

I AM Enough!

As a parent, the best thing one can do is give support and lots of love. Create a space that your child can feel comfortable in, a secure and stable foundation they can call home. As time goes by, many questions will arise, so be prepared. Honesty is the best policy. It establishes trust. When you can have trust, it bridges a connection to be open. You are creating space for open communication.

There is nothing that can prepare mothers for parenting teens. Sure, we have our own experiences in life, but so often, we must pray our children do not have to learn the lessons we did. Raising healthy teens involves a level of structure. The structure creates a sense of security, safety, and consistency.

We spoke about communication in the previous paragraph. Communication is key when establishing structure and revisiting any new rules within any relationship. To a teen, structure may be misunderstood or feel like restrictions. So be careful that you are communicating in each other's language. Here is a book reference I would like to mention for you to learn more about languages. But before I mention the book, I want you to understand why I found it a good reference. It was written by Gary Chapman. I briefly read this book as a teen. I got the five points I needed to heal some inner wounds, and it pushed me in the direction of better understanding myself and others. The book title is *The Five Love Languages* by Gary Chapman.

Why is this important for you and your adolescent, or you and your parents? Well, if you can relate to the story I started with, then it is likely you can find the answer you seek in a book. So it looks like you are off to a great start. Apply the action to activate improvement.

The ABCs of Raising a Healthy, Happy, and Responsible Teen on Their Way to Adulthood

The ABCs of raising a healthy, happy, and responsible teen are **A.** Affirm, **B.** Boundaries, **C.** Communication.

- **Affirm** tour love, and express love in everything you do. Affirm this in action and, indeed, practice daily affirmation. Go out and show love to others. Sometimes we go through things that seem bigger than us. Take the time to stop and do for others. Showing action of service can open our hearts to love in all its essence. How can you show love to someone today? How can you show more love to yourself?

- **Boundaries** What boundaries need to be set in place to build character discipline and identity? Boundaries are non-negotiable. They help you keep yourself and others in alignment with your core values. They are the messages you send out that teach others how to treat you. Here are some categories you can overview as you set boundaries as a guideline to create healthy relationships: self-care, faith, family, finance, career, and friends.

- **Communication** Communication is important for all relationships. Many times, it is not what we say but how we say things. Or how what we say is interpreted by the receiver. Here are the types of communication: verbal, nonverbal, written, and visual. Communication pairs well with how we learn and retain things. Understanding how a person learns will help you deliver a more effective message. Nonverbal communication is received through gestures, movements, motions, and facial expressions. If you pay attention, you can pick up when a person is lying, thinking, excited, sad, or angry, all by observing their body language. Written communication. The most beautiful words are written down on paper, script, and tablet. For years, we write out to-do lists. We write down important dates to remember. We can communicate on paper when spoken words have failed us.

I remember graduating from high school, and shortly after, I was abandoned by my parent. I was starting my first semester in college, and I was left to take care of two siblings, run a household, attend school, and work my nine-to-five. We won't go into the challenges I faced during these times. What I want to highlight is how I was able to communicate through writing all my bottled-up emotions down I had as a child to that parent. It also allowed the parent to communicate all the things they felt uncomfortable saying aloud. At the end of that chapter, we both came out of that situation understanding each other's perspectives and viewpoints. We taught each other from a different angle.

Let me conclude by saying, healing from past trauma, mending bonds, creating trust within yourself, and trusting others is all a process on this journey called life. To create healthy teens who are ready to take on this world, help them establish a close relationship with who you believe in. Let your example of love come from the source. Set boundaries to build up good morals and character. Communicate in a healthy way, in a way that the receiver can understand. Apply the ABC principles toward raising your teen. Nowadays, our youth are on social media and on their phones texting. So there are many ways to get messages of communication across these days.

Visual Learners

Is your child a visual learner? Visual learners learn through seeing something done, so they learn from the way you show up daily through your actions. A visual learner is much different than an auditory learner, and visual learners will understand messages through video pictures and can retain information better in these forms. Create teachable moments while sharing a movie, social media post, or YouTube video. They are all great ways to get your point across when communicating with a visual learner.

One thing I enjoy doing is finding relatable content from other wise counsels and sharing it with my teens. It is a wonderful way to have an open dialogue, but also when they hear the point that you have been trying to prove from someone else, they suddenly get it. It is like a light bulb is switched on. Sometimes a useful resource makes a world of difference. Who are you listening to? So often, we find ourselves in a situation where it seems like we are the only ones in the world going through it. But we aren't the only ones in our environment. Find who speaks to your soul. Who helps you with your growth and development? Apply the lessons being taught by those wise counsels to see continuous growth. I come from a time when it takes a village to raise a child. However, the world may seem a little different these days. Our villages, our community, and our resources are now accessible at the click of a finger. Other times we develop the community we want to see around us. Find community and allow them to help you in the process of raising your team into adulthood. Help your teen find a community that can help them be raised with good manners and as responsible citizens of the world.

Reference: Holy Bible, Jeremiah 1:5

Jason Thibodeaux Bio

Jason Thibodeaux, a native of Houston, Texas, grew up knowing that he wanted to be an entertainer starting at a young age. As Jason grew, so did his personality. It often sparked interest and had him in the spotlight. He has performed in high school and college marching bands and behind the scenes in sound and lighting for stage productions as well as film. He stepped out of the sound and lighting booth and onto the main stage, where he has given awe-inspiring and emotionally jarring performances.

Jason has been featured in several films as well as stage productions such as *The Sons We Were Meant to Be, A Right to Preach, Christmas with the In-Laws* parts I and II, *Retribution, Do's and Don'ts of Dating,* and *VI* the series, written and directed by some of Houston's finest writers and directors. He starred in the feature film *Can You Hear Me?* and directed and starred in the feature film *Pawns.* He helped write the feature film *Karma,* in which he made a cameo appearance. Jason became a published author penning a chapter in the book *The Race to the Ring, The Seven C's to a Successful Relationship* and a chapter in the Amazon #1 best-selling *Why He Married Her &*

Played Me, The Sequel. Jason's resume continues to grow due to his strong integrity and drive, and he hasn't shown signs of slowing!

IMDBPro JasonThibodeax (II)

CHAPTER 8

Teens And Sex

By
Jason Thibodeaux

—————— ⚜ ——————

If you are reading this, then chances are you are a parent or are considering being a parent. If that is the case, you most likely had sex at some point in your teenage or adult years. Sex can be a beautiful thing, a weapon, or abused. In either case, you can consider it a ying to a yang. Let me explain. I'll start backward in this instance.

When sex is abused, it will most likely leave the abused individual in a mental and emotional spiral in which they will either hate the mere thought of the act, use the act to feel loved, or use the act to abuse others. The danger of using the act to feel loved is the person usually will have sex to help fill an empty void in their lives, leading them to have sex repeatedly, with multiple partners, in an attempt to find someone/something to finally make them feel loved or whole.

This opens the individual to disappointment, including sexually transmitted diseases or pregnancy. A conversation about pregnancy goes without needing to go into a deep explanation due to common knowledge and an empty person having difficulty pouring into a child needing attention and love. In regard to contracting a sexually transmitted disease, an abused person looking for love and having sex with multiple partners will find themselves more down on life due to the infections adding to their emptiness. They are usually willing to spread the contracted disease without a care in the world about who they infect.

When sex is used as a weapon, the individual will use the act as a control mechanism. This person will have sex with someone for some type of gain. This gain could be monetary or a manipulative action, a way to entice their partner to do something they most likely would not do if not for the chance to have sex with them. This could be anything from a trip to the shopping mall, trips out of town, expensive meals they can't afford, etc. Like the abused individual, this person can easily be seen as a dangerous person, as love is rarely behind the actual act of sex. The individual has what I like to call an *empty soul*, and sex is merely an act one uses to get something in return. I like to view these individuals as prostitutes, as there is always some sort of monetary exchange or gain, whether directly or indirectly.

Now, when sex is used as the beautiful act it was meant to be, love and care are involved with their partner. One partner is selected at a time (think dating), and the individual is usually looking for a long-time mate. The person is not worried about how many people they can sleep with and are looking for a husband/wife. I will not sugarcoat this act, as this person could come into contact and contract a sexually transmitted disease while dating as with the other individuals above. Any time a person has sex, they can contract an STD. Period, point-blank. However, this individual will usually select their partner more wisely due to their ultimate goal (marriage) and generally will not be as careless while dating and/or having sex.

Subconscious Mind

This chapter is about the struggles between parents and teens and sexuality. If you noticed, I did not address the gender of the person looking to have sex or the gender of the person they are planning to have sex with. I have always said, when you know better, you do better. When you make mistakes, you should learn from them and do all you can to prevent your children and loved ones from making the same mistakes. I often wonder why the topic of sex is so taboo in the eyes of adults when it comes to their teenage children. We were all teenagers once and should remember the challenges and emotional rollercoasters we experienced at that time. As a father of two daughters, one a high school senior at seventeen years old and one a sixth-grader at twelve years old, I can definitely say that I find myself in an interesting space. I often imagine how I would think and handle this subject if I was the father of a son or two. As I stated earlier, when you know better, you do better. My understanding of sex when I was a teenager and my understanding now is completely different, especially as I have matured and created little humans of my own.

My background is similar to most, especially growing up as a teen through the late '80s and '90s. This is the age of *gangsta rap*, the dawn of 2 Live Crew and the genre of music that spawned from these groups. Don't get me wrong, as a musician and lover of music, I completely understand the message in a lot of older music of the late '70s and early '80s and even older when you actually listen to the lyrics of the artists of these time periods. Every decade of music had artists that were explicit for their time period and made waves with their sexually charged music. These days an artist like Ray Charles would be considered old and docile; however, his music was considered very sexually charged during his rise to success.

Now, back to when I was a teen, all of the boys were trying to prove their manhood by actually getting a young lady to allow them to explore sexual acts. Dads pushed their sons to be "real" men, and ladies warned their daughters of these young perverts trying to entice them out of their panties. It could easily be considered somewhat of a toxic time. As gangs really exploded (pushing aggressive sexual acts), the spotlight was on pimps and players (playas) in the hood (belittling the emotional connection to sexual partners), decent neighborhoods were now being overrun with drugs (which loosed inhibitions towards sex), and the music of the time was turning very sexually explicit. Enter the time period of the explicit warning sticker on hip-hop, R&B albums, and beyond. Dancing became way more provocative than in years past, and how the two sexes danced on each other more physically (bumping and grinding) was the new norm.

Sex was becoming more mainstream by leaps and bounds, and what was socially acceptable became more relaxed. What seemed to be a substantial increase in teen pregnancies was becoming more widespread in junior high (middle school) and high schools across the world. Well, at least more noticeable and more projected on television. High schools across several communities started having to purchase and install trailers outside of main school buildings to house teen mothers (and some fathers) trying to continue their education. If we were noticing the shift in thinking and what was becoming more socially acceptable to talk about twenty-five to thirty years ago, imagine the outlook on sex and what is socially acceptable now. Now there is more emphasis on gender roles, gender (LGBTQ), and what is binary and what is not. Lyrics in songs now would have never made it on public radio stations, even a couple of decades ago.

Why am I bringing up music? Music has a direct correlation to thought processes and also what people deem socially acceptable. For example: in the '80s, the beginning of mainstream rap, the artists spoke about parties, getting an education, falling in love (getting the girl/boy of their dreams), not doing drugs, and just general pride in oneself. The rap of the '90s consisted of gangsta rap, positive hip-hop artists, having to sell drugs just to make it, getting out of the hood, self-pride, shaking your backside (butt), getting an education, and well . . . getting as much sex as you can. All of this depended on what genre you listened to. I believe this decade of rap was the most diverse, as there were positive and negative messages. Even a lot of the gangsta rap was politically motivated and told tales of what was happening in more impoverished neighborhoods.

Now the early 2000s started a shift in rap music. Now you have artists speaking about partying, blowing money like it is not a thing, not caring about anything or anyone, staying fly (again blowing money), strip clubs, drug usage, sex (not just sex, but unprotected sex), money over women/men, no self-pride (read: selling oneself for the money, no school, no education, dropping out), everyone's a gangsta now (so they say).

Enter the 2010s and beyond. To me, this is one of the most destructive time periods in rap music as a genre. Most of these rappers are strongly promoting drug usage (often recording music slurring and not pronouncing actual words, high), unprotected sex, internet beefs, shootings (i.e., telling on themselves via social media), no pride in the culture, education, and beyond. This is the time period of not caring about anything or anyone, fake gangstas, etc. This is a very destructive time in music, and music moves a culture. Music also infiltrates the subconscious mind and pushes thoughts, feelings, and what people deem socially acceptable. Now you are thinking, well, I won't let my teens listen to rap music, so they won't be subjected to sexually explicit lyrics and anecdotes. Please understand all other genres follow what rap and hip-hop culture push. So R&B, pop, country music, etc., have all had similar changes and promote similar messages. The same goes for what is now acceptable and shown on television. With the growth of cable TV over the years and now internet TV, what is available and socially acceptable has shifted. Current parents were subjected to this sexualization in entertainment, and they are hypersensitive to anything explicit.

Emotional Maturity

I believe one of the challenges and/or fights of every parent has been how to protect my teen from their hormones and wants to grow up fast? It does not matter whether the parent was promiscuous at an early age; the general consensus is that most parents want their teens to wait to have sex. If the teen starts down the path of being promiscuous, there are chances the teen will become pregnant or create a pregnancy if the teen is male. Sex can cloud judgment for the betterment of self and can deter personal growth. This is because the parent is still taking care of the teen; i.e., the teen is not grown or self-sufficient to take care of a baby or even themselves. The other side of the coin is emotional maturity. Most teens have challenges effectively expressing their feelings. In the past couple of decades, I have noticed teens have a really hard time expressing themselves verbally and usually shift to physical forms of expression. The growth of social media has exacerbated this phenomenon even more. People have seemingly lost the ability to want to communicate outside of their electronic devices and social media. I have pushed for years for my daughters, as well as all of the high school boys that I have mentored, to be able to talk their problems and challenges out as opposed to shutting down and/or expressing themselves physically.

Ownership

The biggest challenge with teens and sex that I have seen is the lack of emotional maturity. The lack of being able to make and handle adult situations can be a taxing game for any teen. Most adults can't seem to handle adult situations well, and we are supposed to be the mature beings! If you notice, we all have friends and family members that go in and out of relationships with emotional baggage and wreak havoc on the new relationship because they never dealt with their emotional health from the relationships that hurt them. (Something to think about.) Another factor in introducing sex to any relationship is that it alters your thinking. Yes, thinking. Once sex is introduced to a relationship, the way you think about that person, the things they do, and the way they make you feel all change. So things your boyfriend/girlfriend once did that would not bother you now become a big problem! It is no longer all fun and games and is not acceptable within the relationship. What am I referring to? A form of possession! Now that sex is introduced, people generally form an attachment to their sexual partner and do not want anyone around them.

You are now wholly theirs, and no one should get the attention your new sexual partner desires. Possession is dangerous, and a lot of people lose their lives daily due to this emotion. If you are wondering why I refer to this as an emotion, it is simple: no one owns anyone! A husband does not own his wife. The wife does not own the husband. So what makes you feel you own a boyfriend or girlfriend because you shared yourself with this person? If people who have pledged their lives to each other have no real ownership of their spouse and have to work daily to please and get along with this person, what makes you feel you own someone you are merely dating? Remember, not just possession, but love in itself is just an emotion. Most feel a sense of love once sex is introduced into the relationship. When not controlled, these emotions will cause challenges in any relationship, all the way down to a simple friendship. One of the items my business partner and I speak about regularly is human emotion and how things seem to change in relationships once titles and sex are involved. It always seems the relationship becomes more work and tenser once titles are involved. This tension and more work grow exponentially once sex is involved.

Parenting

As parents, we all know teens will do what teens do. We all were once teens and got away with whatever we could. Now in the height of social media and cell phones, teens and younger kids have almost unlimited access to all kinds of adult material in the palm of their hands. Kids these days learn how to work a tablet before they can read or write. A positive here, parents also have more access to the whereabouts of their children once they leave the house. Back in my day, we left the house and usually didn't return until the streetlights were about to come on, meaning parents just knew their teen was somewhere in the neighborhood. Now the parent can know the exact location of their teen (I never met a teen that left their phone at the house 😊). If the parent is actually parenting and not allowing the TV or neighborhood to raise their teen, the parent can do a lot to help prevent the teen from engaging in sexual acts. If the parent is not watching or paying attention to their teen, there is a high likelihood their teen has been sexually active for a while. The message here is to get overly involved in your children's day-to-day activities. Especially your teenage children's.

Adulthood

Let's discuss the real reason all teens consider being sexually active. I've mentioned emotions several times within this chapter, so I will not beat a dead horse. Teens consider having sex for the same reason a baby will learn how to walk; the same reason a preteen wants to change their hair or learn to ride a bike; the same reason a teenager wants to learn how to drive: to be an adult. Since our age of understanding, we strive to become an adult as fast as we can. It is like we are missing something in our lives, wanting something, only to get it, and then we wish we would have waited to experience it. Think about it: how often have you made the statement, I wish I was back in high school, or I wish I were in college again? It is human nature to want to grow up fast and have adult life experiences. However it is not until you become grown and must support yourself that you start to understand the respect becoming an adult brings. Then you make the statement that you want to go back to being a teen and start over, do it again, and enjoy an easier life.

Know Better, Do Better

Before, I often imagined how I would think and handle this subject if I was the father of a son or two. I also stated that when you know better, you do better. Let's just be honest, no parent, especially a father, wants his teen daughter sexually active. But to be honest, I would feel the same way if I had sons. Things are different these days, perceptions, political correctness, what is socially acceptability, etc.

As a parent and community advocate, I don't want any teen to engage in sexual activity.

I don't want any young adult to engage in sexual activity until that young adult is emotionally mature and can handle the emotions and challenges that come with the act of sex. Adults can't seem to handle and process adult activities.

So again, when we know better, we do better.

Victoria Jones DuBose Bio

Lady Victoria loves writing. It has been her passion since her teenage years. Her first published works were some of her poems and short stories. Her journalistic training began at Columbia College, Chicago, where she initially majored in broadcast journalism but later switched her major to writing journalism. In 2012, Lady Victoria participated in her first anthology project, becoming an author of the best-selling book *Race to the Ring, The Seven C's of s Successful Courtship*. Lady Victoria is happy to present to you this first publication, *Teens and Broken Homes*, a series of The Parenting and Teens Anthology Project.

When Lady Victoria is not writing, she is teaching and coaching dining etiquette and lifestyle skills to teenagers and adults. Her etiquette curriculum focuses on sharpening individuals' personal and professional manners within their private and public spheres of influence. Additionally, Lady Victoria runs a mentorship program for tweens and teenagers centered on self-esteem, self-love, and personal growth and development.

CHAPTER 9

Teens And Broken Homes

By
Victoria Jones DuBose Meet the Synclair's

———————— ❦ ————————

arcie Synclair grew up in an affluent family living in the posh suburban town of Caledonia. Her parents' baby mansion of a home was impressive with its thirteen rooms, long winding staircase, and enormous, beautiful chandeliers on almost every level. Even the doorknobs in every room looked like polished gold. She and her two brothers, William and Henry, were doted on by their parents for as long as Marcie could remember. The house cleaners came weekly to ensure their home was always spotless. Their chef was the envy of her parents' friends, who were always trying to steal him away from them. As a teenager, Marcie and her brothers no longer had the need for nannies or caretakers (she and her brothers referred to them as "shadows"), but their butler made it a sneaky little habit to pop up whenever they were out of sight or sound for too long. Marcie and her friends had regular daily routines that they followed to the letter. School, gymnastics, dance, and a healthy bite to eat before the family chauffeur dropped Marcie's friends and herself at home. She and her friends had known each other all their lives and lived in the same community as well. It was normal for the chauffeurs to rotate weeks of picking the girls up from their favorite little cafe and dropping them off at their various homes.

Marcie's mom, Frieda, owned a high-end jewelry shop on the other end of town. Marcie's older brother, William, usually picked up Frieda from the jewelry shop, while the younger Henry typically arrived home just ahead of Marcie. Her Dad, Douglas, operated his business from his central office in the center of the hustle and bustle of the West-End Business Sector, downtown in the city. Douglas enjoyed riding the commuter train into suburbia and was met at the station by the family chauffeur for the twenty-minute ride home. They all returned home before dinner, seizing the opportunity to chat up their day as their chef was prepared to serve dinner within the hour. Yes, everything about their life and home was perfectly perfect until it no longer was.

Defining Broken Homes

According to the most recently available Census Bureau Report[10] 2008–2012, 56 percent of families in America with teenagers between the ages of fifteen and seventeen years old come from what is defined as a *broken home*. Two reliable dictionary sources, the *Oxford* and *Merriam-Webster Dictionaries*[11] , respectively ascribe the definitions of a broken home as "a family where the parents are separated or divorced," "a family where the parents have divorced."

These two sources provide such a broad description of the term *broken home* that it almost seems applicable to any teenager living with at least one biological parent. It is my opinion that both definitions chose to define broken homes using only the top three reasons why families may end up as

---

10 United States Census Bureau, 2008-2012

2 The Oxford and Merriam-Webster Dictionaries

broken homes. Dictionaries are purposefully concise with the content they print. After all, words are an ongoing evolution that changes with time and cultures. Diving deeper into my research, I found myself searching for something meatier to support what was already deep in my spirit. I have memories of broken homes that mirrored the definitions of a lot of what I had seen in families with single, separated, divorced parents raising their children. I have also witnessed the intact nuclear family dealt the same hand as the single, separated, divorced family. What makes these people different? Different classes of people living out the same experiences; no, that definition had to be there as well. Through no choice of my own, I had witnessed the broken family and the nuclear family with my own eyes come tumbling down. It was not a pretty sight. I was in the room when it happened, living the experience as if it were my own. The pressure, hurt, defeat, and pain; it does not subside quickly nor easily dissipate. Not everyone fits the descriptions defined above. Some people are whole until the complexities of life and love turn into massive tidal waves they never saw coming. Hurt and pain soon find an unwelcome comfort in depression.

Broken homes do not just happen. Broken homes are comprised of broken people. These people may not have started out this way but ended up there for reasons that are as varied as there are snowflakes. No two are the same.

Dr. Frank Anderson, a psychiatrist and psychotherapist specializing in the treatment of traumas, had this to say about broken families: "A broken family is one that includes unhealthy or severed relationships within the family unit. They are often associated with divorce but certainly can occur in an intact family where various members are in conflict with or estranged from each other."[12] Anderson further explains that there are a variety of reasons why the classes of people do not really matter when it comes to broken families. Estrangement can happen for several reasons: mental health issues, abuse, illness, overly controlling parents, crossing barriers, different belief systems,[13] and the list goes on. Some adult parents may not have the same capacity to rear children

---

12 Frank Anderson, MD, Psychiatrist, and Psychotherapist.

13 Very Well Mind, "Having a Broken Family: What It Means and How to Cope," Frank Anderson, MD.

as effectively as others, even though they have been doing so for several years. It is not for outsiders to make the judgment call of pass or fail, right or wrong. In these tumultuous situations, people learn to adapt in ways that may not be effective for you or me, but it works for them and even sometimes works for their families. This can be true for the intact family as well as the broken family. Brokenness shows no prejudicial preferences. We are all susceptible to it. The children are the real victims in these cases. Without some intervention, therapy, or counseling, these children grow up angry, fearful, sometimes isolated, and reserved. It is about the age of twenty-five years that the adult learns how to control their anger and emotions. It is unfair to expect an abused child turned teenager to understand in any way what is happening to them, let alone know how to manage the anger and emotions they are feeling at the same time. We must consider, above all things, the impact that brokenness has not just on the individual but the family unit as well.

Marcie's Story

Marcie Synclair and her family were a close-knit family. She loved her brothers intensely and thought she could never disappoint or refuse them anything. She knew that they felt the same way about her too. Her being the middle child did not affect her as it typically would have affected other middle children. She thought nothing could ever come between them or their parents. She trusted them implicitly.

Henry was going to be seventeen this summer, and this little brother had grown into quite the handsome young man. William was already collaborating part time with their dad, Douglas, downtown after his early classes, leaving Henry with more spare time on his hands. Marcie could not say that Henry was chasing girls, as many times some of Henry's female classmates or friends of friends drove by to say hello or plainly invite Henry for coffee, brunch, parties, or just a drive to fill in some of their free time. Marcie sometimes giggled to herself, knowing the girls were doing much more chasing Henry than he them. Oh well, he was just doing what William had done a couple of summers ago, so Henry would be simply fine. After a few weeks, Henry preferred Sarah Jane Peters, who never came to visit Henry, but traveled in the same circles as many of the girls who did visit Henry. Henry and Sarah Jane sure were spending a lot of time together lately. Henry shared with Marcie how special Sarah Jane was to him and how he was always looking to impress her. He could not imagine ever hurting Sarah Jane.

A few weeks after that conversation, Henry told Marcie that Sarah Jane would be leaving for college a year early because she had been accepted into a special program at her college because of her consistent 4.0 GPA throughout high school. He could not fathom being without Sarah Jane for more than a few days, let alone an entire year! Marcie decided to take her brother out to cheer him up the week Sarah Jane left. Marcie was a bit surprised at Henry's somber mood. It was not at all like him to behave this way.

On the drive home, Marcie suggested that they stop by the pond they used to play at when they were kids. As they walked along the path, Marcie grabbed Henry's hand like she used to when they were kids. It was several hours later before

Marcie and Henry returned home to their beautiful mansion. Marcie knew that Jorge, their butler heard them come in. Marcie and Henry were glad that Jorge did not leave his quarters to greet them home. They both went straight to their rooms with mumbled goodnights.

It has been one year since Marcie and Henry walked by the childhood pond holding hands.

William now runs the family business with the help of the board and guidance and direction from two or three of Douglas's longtime partners. William is determined to finish his MA in business administration and communications. Henry left for the Air Force months ago. Frieda sold her jewelry boutique to her best customer for less than half of what she should have gotten for it.

The Synclair family now has new house cleaners. Their prized chef came with them when they moved into their new countryside home. Jorge, the butler, runs the countryside home with the same finesse and precision as when they lived in Caledonia. Bloomington is beautiful with all its gardens, parks, and water fountains. Marcie misses her friends. She can face them again in time, but she does not think she is quite ready yet. It is still stressful having to deal with the trauma of it all. Her dad hugs her all the time, but now more like she is a china doll instead of his beautiful daughter. He has lost his vibrancy and zest for life. His phone became his office, but only when he could bring himself to face the real world out there. She can hear her parents crying in each other's arms at night. She tries to tell them repeatedly that none of this was their fault. It has been a terrible tragedy for them all, an unforeseen tragedy that no one could have predicted. Marcie knows how much it would have cost them to keep up pretenses in Caledonia. She thinks to herself, maybe it will become too much for her one day too.

Marcie gathers her wits about herself. She has taught herself not to think about it too much. She has awful migraines when she does. Marcie asks the chef to prepare a pitcher of her favorite fruit tea and bring it out to the garden. She has decided she will read her favorite book of poetry at her infant son's garden grave. No one would guess it was a gravesite because of all the flowers. Her precious little baby boy blends right in with all the sweet and luscious odors amongst the vibrant colors and fertile soil. Marcie reads her poetry in a sing-song voice, sipping her iced tea in between verses. Halfway through the poetry book and the fruit tea, Marcie decides it is time to go upstairs and cry herself to sleep.

If you or someone you know is suffering from depression, mental health or needs mental health support, please call the National Depression Hotline at: (866) 903-3787.

If you or someone you know is suffering from substance abuse, please call SAMHSA at 1-800- 662 HELP (4357).

If you or someone you know is suffering from post-partum depression, please call or text the Post-Partum Support Hotline at: (800) 273-TALK (8255).

If you or someone you know is suffering sexual assault or needs to report a rape or sexual trauma, or needs to talk with support staff, please call RAIIN at (800) 656 HOPE.

__PLEASE REACH OUT TO GET THE HELP YOU NEED TO SURVIVE AND THRIVE!__

KOFFE10K.COM

Coach P.
KOFFE BROWN
VISIONARY & CHIEF EXECUTIVE
OFFICER

832-510-9193

We hope you have enjoyed this presentation. For more information, writing, publishing and coaching sessions go to

www.koffe10k.com.

www.ingramcontent.com/pod-product-compliance
Lightning Source LLC
Chambersburg PA
CBHW032056040426
42335CB00036B/408